# Crescent City Snow

## The Ultimate Guide to

### NEW ORLEANS SNOWBALL STANDS

*To The Village. I couldn't have done it without you. You loyal.
I like that. That's a major key.*

*In memory of Dr. Michael Mizell-Nelson, the Poorboyologist.
I wish you were here to laugh about snowball vs. snoball vs.
sno-ball with me. Thank you for believing in me and for inspiring me. Without you, I doubt I'd be here.*

http://ulpress.org
University of Louisiana at Lafayette Press
P.O. Box 40831
Lafayette, LA 70504-0831

# Crescent City Snow

## The Ultimate Guide to

## NEW ORLEANS SNOWBALL STANDS

Megan Braden-Perry

2017

UNIVERSITY OF LOUISIANA AT LAFAYETTE PRESS

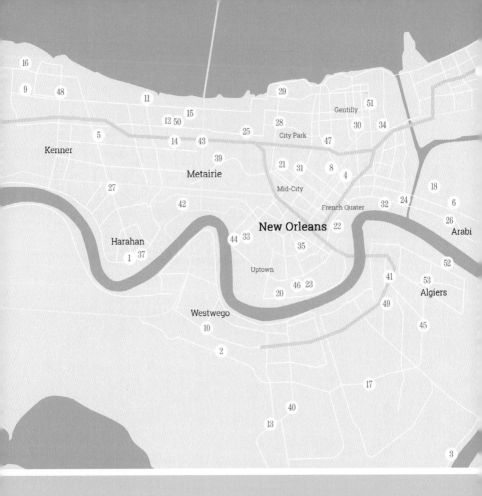

1 ABear's Snoball Stand

2 Abracadabra Snowballs

3 Belle Chasse Dairy Dip

4 Big Chief Snowballs

5 The Big Chill

6 Blizzard Balls

7 Brain Freeze

8 Broad Street Snowballs

9 Bubbie's Sno-Balls & Ice Cream

10 Buck's Sno-Wiz

11 Casey's Snowballs

12 Chilly's Snoballs

13 Cold Spot

14 Dino's Sno-balls & Ice Cream

15 Fat City Snoballs

16 Flavors Snoballs

17 The Frigid Zone Sno-Balls

18 Galvez Goodies

# New Orleans
## Snowball Stands Map

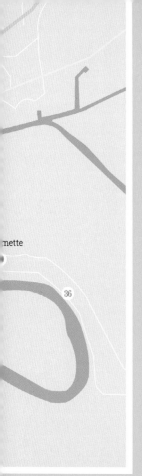

27 Mr. Frank's Snoballs

28 NOLA Snow

29 NOLA Snow (second location)

30 The Original New Orleans Snoball & Smoothie

31 Pandora's Snowballs

32 Piety Street Sno-Balls

33 Plum Street Snoballs

34 Pontilly Sno

35 Red Rooster Snowballs

36 River Breez Sno Balls

37 Ro-Bear's

38 Rodney's

39 Sal's Sno-Balls

40 Scuba Steve's

41 Shivering Sam's Snowballs

42 Sno Shak

43 Sno-La Snoball Lounge

44 Sno-La Snoball Lounge (second location)

45 Snow World Sno-balls

46 SnoWizard Snoball Shoppe

47 Stop Jockin Sno-Ball Stand

48 Sunny's

49 Sweet Shack Snowballs

50 Taft Park Snoballs

51 Taste This! Snowballs

52 Van's Snoballs

53 Van's Snoballs (second location)

54 Who Want Some

19 Goody's Sno-Balls

20 Hansen's Sno-Bliz

21 Ike's Snowballs

22 Imperial Woodpecker Sno-Balls

23 Imperial Woodpecker Sno-Balls (second location)

24 Lickety Split's Sweet Shop

25 Lou-Lou's Snoballs & Ice Cream

26 Mom & Pop Snowballs and Hot Tamales

# TABLE OF CONTENTS

ABear's Snoball Stand ..................................................................... 1

Abracadabra Snowballs ..................................................................... 5

Belle Chasse Dairy Dip ..................................................................... 9

Big Chief Snowballs ..................................................................... 13

The Big Chill ..................................................................... 17

Blizzard Balls ..................................................................... 21

Brain Freeze ..................................................................... 25

Broad Street Snowballs ..................................................................... 29

Bubbie's Sno-Balls & Ice Cream ..................................................................... 33

Buck's Sno-Wiz ..................................................................... 37

Casey's Snowballs ..................................................................... 41

Chilly's Snoballs ..................................................................... 45

Cold Spot ..................................................................... 49

Dino's Sno-balls & Ice Cream ..................................................................... 53

Fat City Snoballs ..................................................................... 57

Flavors Snoballs ..................................................................... 61

The Frigid Zone Sno-Balls ..................................................................... 65

Galvez Goodies ..................................................................... 69

Goody's Sno-Balls ..................................................................... 73

Hansen's Sno-Bliz ..................................................................... 77

Ike's Snowballs ..................................................................... 81

Imperial Woodpecker Sno-Balls ..................................................................... 85

Lickety Split's Sweet Shop ..................................................................... 89

Lou-Lou's Snoballs & Ice Cream ..................................................................... 93

Mom & Pop Snowballs and Hot Tamales ..................................................................... 97

Mr. Frank's Snoballs ............................................................. 101

NOLA Snow ............................................................................ 105

The Original New Orleans Snoball & Smoothie ................. 109

Pandora's Snowballs ............................................................. 113

Piety Street Sno-Balls .......................................................... 117

Plum Street Snoballs ............................................................ 121

Pontilly Sno ........................................................................... 125

Red Rooster Snowballs ......................................................... 129

River Breez Sno Balls ........................................................... 133

Ro-Bear's ............................................................................... 137

Rodney's ................................................................................. 141

Sal's Sno-Balls ...................................................................... 145

Scuba Steve's ......................................................................... 149

Shivering Sam's Snowballs .................................................. 153

Sno Shak ................................................................................. 157

Sno-La Snoball Lounge ........................................................ 161

Snow World Sno-balls .......................................................... 165

SnoWizard Snoball Shoppe .................................................. 169

Stop Jockin Sno-Ball Stand ................................................. 173

Sunny's ................................................................................... 177

Sweet Shack Snowballs ........................................................ 181

Taft Park Snoballs ................................................................ 185

Taste This! Snowballs ........................................................... 189

Van's Snoballs ....................................................................... 193

Who Want Some ..................................................................... 197

# introduction

All interviewees for this book were asked the same three questions: Do you have any fun or interesting memories tied to snowballs? Do you always get this flavor at this stand? What flavors and stands did you grow up with?

Almost always, folks said they started with bubble gum, strawberry, or other "kiddie flavors" but matured into wedding cake, nectar, and other more sophisticated flavors. Most people visit their neighborhood snowball stands or the stands near their schools, with the "green house by Brother Martin" being my interviewees' most frequented stand. As for memories, most people I interviewed remember going after school or summer camp with their families. But hardly anyone remembers the names of the stands. They'll remember locations—even family members' flavors—but rarely stand names.

Coconut coffee snowball from Who Want Some

I also learned there's no flavor like spearmint, and people either love or hate having blue bubble gum-stained mouths.

Wild cherry with condensed milk snowball from Dino's

Banana-caramel soft serve
from Pontilly Sno

Me, I've got a memory like an ele-
phant. I can remember almost every
stand I've visited and almost every
flavor I've tried. (I tried fifty different
flavors for this book!) When the "green
house by Brother Martin" first opened in
the mid-90s, back in my McDonogh No. 39
elementary days, I remember trying the cotton
candy flavor with my grownup cousin Chuck Braden and telling
him it tasted like "the drink Uncle H.E. drank." "Jack Daniels?!"
he asked. "YES! That's it!" And we agreed it DID taste like Jack.

My Paw Paw would always get pineapple and strawberry,
telling me that in his Gilbert Academy days the girls would get
that and say, "Red and yella, catch a fella!"

And at this one snowball stand on Gentilly, where Burger
Orleans is now, my best friend Allen Haynes's brother Demitri
ordered a Hurricane snowball. We were
all still in elementary school, so I
thought we were being so cool
and rebellious. Then there
were those times when I
was a high school student
at Ben Franklin and would
ask my Paw Paw to take
my best friend Erica Wiltz
and I to the Brother Mar-
tin snowball stand, where

Pineapple upside down cake
snowball from the Cold Spot

X

she always wanted to coordinate her snowball with her outfit. I once tripped over the roots of the tree out front and was so embarrassed. And when I was at Lusher Extension for middle school, I felt so very cool sneaking to walk to Plum Street after school with Uptown natives like Eddie Brown.

Now that I'm older, my favorite thing about snowballs is that they are icy, sweet tokens of affection. You can show your feelings for someone better with a snowball than you can with a card. Think of how you felt when a friend brought you a snowball to the hospital, like my friend Erin Johnson did for me? Or when your grandfather picked you up from summer camp and took you for a surprise one? How about when you were on a date and the person you were with remembered what flavor you liked and how you liked it dressed? Or when your mom jooged your snowball for you and sipped a little juice out of it so you wouldn't waste any? Moments like that, I treasure. They are what make snowballs more than just a snack.

Cherry cheesecake snowball with whipped cream and a cherry on top from Goody's

# ABear's
## Snoball Stand

### 121 Westbank Expy., Westwego

· · · · · · · · · · · · · · · · · · · · · ·

**My order:** Who Dat

**Details about stand:** There's a covered area to stand and eat snowballs, and they have a nice selection of flavors, ice cream treats, and snowball stand snacks. There are even frozen pickle shots.

> Working at a snowball stand is fun and you get to meet different people and learn what they like and other fun things about them. We have a lot of regular customers here. We do a huge variety here with banana splits, shakes, nachos. My favorite flavor is the sugar-free pineapple, and when I was a kid it was ice cream with condensed milk. When I was a kid we lived in the country, so we didn't really get too much snowballs.
>
> —Sherry Hodge

**MY THOUGHTS:** My favorite flavor here, one of my favorite snowballs in the greater New Orleans area, is Jamaican man. It tastes like creamy tropical fruit and is a gorgeous melon color. This is a perfect little stand.

# ABRACADABRA
## SNOWBALLS

1309 Lapalco Blvd., Westwego
(504) 669-5280
www.facebook.com/Abracadabrasnow

**MY ORDER:** Reese's cup

**DETAILS ABOUT STAND:** The stand is covered with plenty of space to stand and eat. There are always a few fun novelty snowballs, like the red velvet stuffed with real red velvet cake. Ice cream treats and normal snowball stand foods are also sold.

> I've got diet cotton candy. I used to always get sour apple, wedding cake, or strawberry. We come to this stand all the time because it has the softest ice and the shortest lines. We try to support the owners. My wife likes stuffed peach, my daughters like coconut, bubble gum, and peach.

### –David Blanchet

> I'm eight now and got red velvet today, but when I was a little boy I used to get coconut. It's also so affordable. When all of us went to the snowball stand for the first time and we all got snowballs, that was really fun.

### –Kwesi Blanchet

**MY THOUGHTS:** Keep up with them on social media to see what fun snowballs they are offering for the moment. They are affordable too, with the fanciest snowballs costing only about four dollars.

# BELLE CHASSE
## Dairy Dip

### 9252 Highway 23, Belle Chasse
### (504) 392-8354

**MY Order:** Bubble gum

**DETAILS ABOUT STAND:** Located on a busy highway in a quiet part of Belle Chasse, this stand offers ample outdoor seating, lots of different flavors, ice cream and ice cream treats, po'boys and other sandwiches, and nachos.

> My favorite flavor snowball is spearmint. I used to not really have a favorite flavor when I was little. I've never really liked ones that were overly sweet. Spearmint kind of evolved into my favorite because it's kinda sweet but it has some complexity with a bit of spice. And I never get anything on it, just plain spearmint.
>
> My dad used to take us to Plum Street when we were little. He never really was one for adventuring, and that place was close to where we lived so that's kinda where we would go. One of the reasons I like spearmint is that it's pretty standard and hard to mess up. I've never had one that was really bad, but there are definitely some that are better than others. I like it when it has a little bit more on the spice side and not just sweet. Sal's is probably my favorite and I like Piety Street, too.
>
> —grant capone

**MY THOUGHTS:** The design of this stand makes my heart flutter, and I feel like I'm on a TV show going to get a bite after a game. The snowball was good, and I hope to try the food soon.

# Big Chief
## snowballs

1739 N. Galvez St., New Orleans
(504) 304-9967
www.facebook.com/bigchiefsnowballs/

**My Order:** Wine cooler

**Details about stand:** I've been passing by this stand since I was little, unless I'm imagining that. It's perfect if you're in the area, say during a second line or leaving Corpus Christi. Bulletproof glass surrounds it, which can make it hard to communicate with employees, but I was raised in this neighborhood so I get why it's there.

> I like granny smith apple, but I like strawberry cheesecake, too. I've been working here since I was like thirteen and I'm eighteen now. When we aren't open, I go to Elysian Fields. Working at a snowball stand has helped me in my other jobs too, like at Sam's where I work now. People come here and like that we have soft ice, so I think it's soft ice, good flavoring.
>
> —TROY HURST

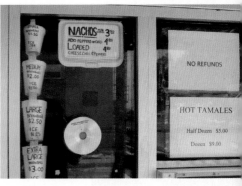

**MY THOUGHTS:** I need to walk around my neighborhood more, so I'll definitely go back. Good snowballs and nice service, I just get a little frustrated feeling like I can neither see nor hear well outside the bulletproof glass. I'd have to go on a day where I have an envie for a certain flavor, so I can just order and go. But I like that there's a patio for me to stand on while I reminisce on my childhood popping in and out of houses on and off London Avenue.

### SNO-BALL FLAVORS

| | | | |
|---|---|---|---|
| ALMOND | COTTON CANDY | LEMON LIME | SPEARMINT |
| BANANA | DAIQUIRI | MARGARITA | STRAWBERRY |
| BLACKBERRY | DREAMSICLE | MANGO | STRAWBERRY SHORTCAKE |
| BLACK CHERRY | GEORGIA PEACH | NECTAR | STRAWBERRY CHEESECAKE |
| BLUEBERRY | GRANNY SMITH APPLE | ORANGE | TANGERINE |
| BUBBLEGUM | GRAPE | PASSION FRUIT | TIGERS BLOOD |
| BUTTERCREAM | HAWAIIAN | PINEAPPLE | TUTTI FRUTTI |
| CAKE BATTER | HULK PUNCH | PINA COLADA | WINE COOLER |
| CAJUN RED HOT | HURRICANE | PINK CHAMPAGNE | VANILLA |
| CHERRY | ICE CREAM | PINK LEMONADE | WATERMELON |
| CHOCOLATE | KIWI | RASPBERRY | WEDDING CAKE |
| COCONUT | LEMON | ROOT BEER | WILD CHERRY |
| OLA | | Praline | |

### CREAM FLAVORS

| | | | |
|---|---|---|---|
| ANANA | CHOCOLATE | HAWAIIAN | PINEAPPLE |
| LUEBERRY | COCONUT | KING CAKE | STRAWBERRY |
| | | PEACH | |

### SNO LITE FLAVORS (SUGAR FREE)

| | | | |
|---|---|---|---|
| NANA | GRAPE | LEMON | PINEAPPLE |
| ERRY | CHOCOLATE | ORANGE | STRAWBERRY |
| | | | WEDDING CAKE |

### TOPPINGS

| | | |
|---|---|---|
| HOCOLATE SYRUP | CONDENSED MILK | ICE CREAM |

NO REFUNDS

HOT TAMALES

Half Dozen  $5.00

Dozen  $9.00

OPEN

# THE BIG CHILL

2413 David Dr., Metairie
(504) 779-6566
www.facebook.com/thebigchillsnowballs

**MY ORDER:** Dulce de leche

**DETAILS ABOUT STAND:** It's right by Lafreniere Park and there's a little seating. What sets this stand apart from the others are the Latin American flavors, including guanabana, tamarindo, dulce de leche, horchata, maracuya, and flan. Credit cards are accepted, and they serve tamales, hot dogs, nachos, ice cream treats, and other little snacks.

Working at a snowball stand is fun, and it's not as simple as it looks. It's not just making a cone and putting it in a cup. It's a lot more demanding. My favorite part is having to eat everything all day. We have a bunch of regulars from all around, even if they're from the Westbank. We have a lot of the Spanish flavors like tamarindo and horchata, and you really don't find that anywhere but here.

My favorite flavor is chocolate, and it's kinda funny because a lot of people's chocolates are different. Ours, we make with Hershey's syrup, and it's just better than anybody else's. When I was little, I loved bubble gum, and I loved ice cream. Those are some of our main flavors. As I grew older, I started to like everything chocolate.

–Karly Masson

**MY THOUGHTS:** The Latin American flavors keep me coming back, especially the ones they serve that are made with real fruit. Hopefully I can try the mango sundae soon. The address says David Drive, but it's kinda set back, behind the car wash. I usually go from behind, as if I'm going to Lafreniere Park.

# BLIZZARD BALLS

7012 W. Judge Perez Dr., Arabi

**MY ORDER:** Tamarind

**DETAILS ABOUT STAND:** This used to be a Honduran snowball stand where you could get Honduran food, but it's changed hands. The ice was a bit crunchy, but the new owner is just getting into the snowball business. The syrups were as they should be, and the stuffed chocolate snowball is their current specialty.

\*Closed as of fall 2016

I always get blue vanilla here, but at other places I get anything red. The color matters to me more than the flavor. The deep blood red is my favorite. When I was a little boy, I loved grape. I keep my snowballs plain with no condensed milk or anything. After school, we'd ride the bikes about a mile down the road in Metairie on Airline to go get snowballs.

—CHARLES POLK

**MY THOUGHTS:** My favorite thing about this snowball stand is watching the traffic go down Judge Perez and sometimes even watching the train. It's breezy, so you can lounge a bit.

# Brain Freeze

10816 Hayne Blvd., New Orleans
(985) 290-5195
www.instagram.com/brainfreezenola

**MY ORDER:** Dreamsicle

**DETAILS ABOUT STAND:** It's attached to Castnet Seafood and Walker's Barbecue and has a covered seating area. They offer your everyday snowballs and sides, perfect for dessert after a hearty lunch or dinner from next door.

> Orchid cream vanilla and wedding cake is the only one that I get. I don't even try any other flavors. No condensed milk, just like this. When I was a kid, it was always pineapple. Snowballs, they make you work out. In fact, I haven't had lunch or anything because I knew I was getting this snowball on the way back to my house in Slidell.
>
> –Brenda Landor

## Brain Freeze

| | | | |
|---|---|---|---|
| NACHOS | $3.50 | EGG ROLLS | |
| W/ CHILI | $4.00 | HALF DOZEN | $4.00 |
| | | | |
| HOT DOG | $1.50 | CRAWFISH/Meat-Pies | |
| W/ CHEESE | $2.00 | 5 for $4.00 | |
| W/ CHILI | $2.00 | w/ fries $5.00 | |
| W/ CHILI & CHEESE | $2.25 | | |
| | | | |
| HOT TAMALES | | | |
| SINGLE | $1.00 | CHICKEN STRIPS | |
| HALF DOZEN | $5.00 | 3 STRIPS | $4.00 |
| DOZEN | $9.00 | W/ FRIES | $5.00 |
| | | | |
| CHIPS | .50¢ | CHICKEN NUGGETS | |
| W/ CHEESE | $1.25 | 10 NUGGETS | $4.00 |
| W/ CHILI | $1.25 | W/ FRIES | $5.00 |

**MY THOUGHTS:** This is one of my favorite places to take friends when they come home to visit, or to bring newcomers to the city. It's got everything you could want as far as New Orleans food: snowballs and sides at the stand, and po'boys, seafood platters, boiled seafood, barbecue, and other traditional New Orleans fare right next door.

| BLACKBERRY | WINE COOLER | LARGE CUP: |
| --- | --- | --- |
| BLACK CHERRY | WHITE RUSSIAN | BROWNIES: $1.00 |
| BLUEBERRY | WILD CHERRY | WITH ICE CREAM: $2.00 |
| BLUE HAWAIIAN | WILD STRAWBERRY | STRAWBERRY |
| BUBBLE GUM | | SHORTCAKE: $3.00 |
| CAKE BATTER | SOUR FLAVORS: | HONEYBUNS: $1.00 |
| CANDY APPLE | SOUR CHERRY | FAMOUS AMOS: .75¢ |
| CHERRY | SOUR GRAPE | |
| COCONUT | SOUR STRAWBERRY | |
| COTTON CANDY | SOUR WATERMELON | |
| DAIQURI | PINK LEMON SOUR | |
| DREAMSICLE | | |
| FUZZIA NAVEL | | |
| GEORGIA PEACH | CLEAR FLAVORS: | $2.25 |
| GRANNY SMITH APPLE | BUBBLE GUM | $1.90 MED |
| GRAPE | GRAPE | |
| HAWAIIAN | SPEARMINT | |
| HURRICANE | STRAWBERRY | |
| ICE-CREAM | | |
| KIWI | SUGARFREE (.25¢): | |
| KING CAKE | ICE CREAM | |
| LEMON LIME | STRAWBERRY | |
| LEMONADE | WEDDING CAKE | $1.75 $2.75 |
| MAGARITA | CHERRY | LRG |
| MANGO | GRANNY SMITH APPLE | |
| MOJITO | PINEAPPLE | |
| NECTAR | | |
| ORANGE | CREAM FLAVORS (.75¢): | |
| PASSON FRUIT | | |
| PINA COLADA | | |

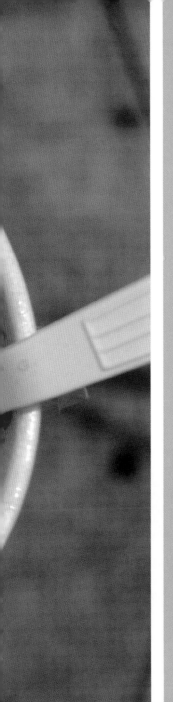

# BROAD STREET
## SNOWBALLS

### 1703 N. Broad St., New Orleans
### (504) 322-2172

**MY ORDER:** Mango and watermelon

**DETAILS ABOUT STAND:** It's on a very busy part of Broad, blocks from St. Bernard, so it's fun to go there and people watch and listen to the St. Aug band practice. And the way they name the sizes is cute: big daddy, big mama, lil mama.

> My favorite flavor snowball is strawberry shortcake because it's sweet but kinda tangy at the same time. I like a mixture of that. I really don't like condensed milk, but a lot of our customers get that flavor with condensed milk.
>
> I used to like bubble gum, but I didn't like my mouth being stained blue for the rest of the day. So I had to change that to red or green. I used to like green apple, especially after football practice. Nothing quenches your thirst better than green apple. But since I'm in a snowball stand in the cool air all day, it allows me to just taste something instead of just trying to quench my thirst. I used to like to go to the one by Brother Martin, but that kinda died off after we opened this one.

– Whitman Wilcox

**MY THOUGHTS:** This stand is within walking distance of my house, so I love the convenience. I can just walk right over with the baby, enjoying the shade from the trees on the block. And the snowballs are really good!

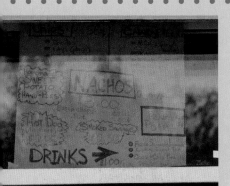

# Bubbie's
## sno-balls & ice cream

391 West Esplanade Ave., Kenner
(504) 305-5504

- - - - - - - - - - - - - - - - - - - - - - - - - -

**My order:** Creole cream cheese

**Details about stand:** There's such a huge variety of flavors at this year-round indoor stand, and in addition to snowballs and traditional snowball stand snacks, they serve bubble tea, ice cream, shakes, and malts. It's also very bright and clean.

> I like tart flavors, so I like either lemon-lime or pink lemonade. Me and my wife used to have our snowball stand back in the 90s, on Jefferson Highway across from Riverdale. You gotta keep the blade sharp to keep your ice real snowy.
>
> Some people short on sugar when they make the simple syrup, so it's not as sweet as the flavor should be. A lot of people will claim they have sugar-free flavors, just because they use the Sno-Lite, but you have to use a syrup that doesn't have sugar in the concentrate for it to be really sugar-free for diabetics. They'll use grape which has the sugar in it, or nectar which has the sugar in it. My wife doesn't want someone who's a diabetic to think they're getting a sugar-free snowball and then wind up having problems. They might not call it sugar-free, they might call it diet, but people see that and think sugar-free.
>
> –Wayne Slaney

MY THOUGHTS: With so many snowball and ice cream flavors and toppings, this is a fun place to experiment and break away from your usual order.

# Buck's Sno-Wiz

133 Westbank Expy., Westwego
www.facebook.com/buckssnowiz

**MY ORDER:** Blueberry cheesecake with whipped cream and seafood boiled potatoes with cheese

**DETAILS ABOUT STAND:** They've got a drive-through with fancy traffic lights, all the standard flavors (and a few hard-to-find ones like Fruitasia and cappuccino), malts, banana splits, floats, and seafood boiled potatoes! There are picnic tables in a covered area outside, and it's right next door to a seafood market.

> This is my first time at Buck's. I live down Barataria, so I go to the Cold Spot usually. I got coconut today, but I always get something different. My top three favorites are cherry, grape, and coconut. I grew up in Gretna and used to go to a stand on Huey P. Long, Castand's. Used to ride my bike and get either grape or orange. The only difference now is that I try to eat the sugar-free ones, since I'm not supposed to have too much sugar. And that when I was a kid, they came in the little paper cups with the pointed bottom.

–KATHY CREATH

**MY THOUGHTS:** Snowball drive-throughs are just amazing to me, especially when you are having a bad day and just need a snowball. Or in this case maybe a banana split and some seafood boiled potatoes. I met the owner (the original owner Buck's daughter) and she explained to me that they get their syrups from different places and that they often mix their own specialty flavors rather than buying them premade. The best thing to me is that they have so many toppings. I'm wondering how a snowball topped with Oreo crumbles would be.

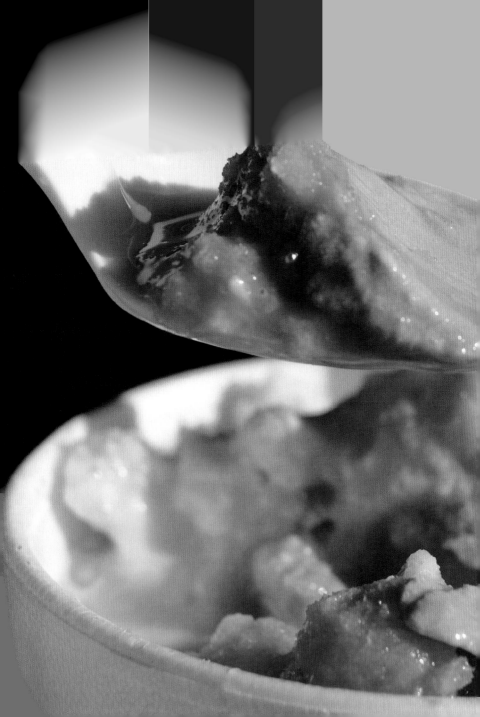

# CASEY'S
## SNOWBALLS

4608 W. Esplanade Ave., Metairie
(504) 888-3920
www.facebook.com/pages/Caseys-Snowballs/

**MY ORDER:** Grasshopper stuffed with chocolate soft serve and topped with condensed milk

**DETAILS ABOUT STAND:** This Metairie institution has a ton of parking and serves snowballs and ice cream treats. They have lots of old school flavors, like Frangelico n' Cream, grasshopper, and old-fashioned nectar cream, but they are famous for their chocolate.

> I've been working at Casey's for three years, and my favorite flavor is chocolate with condensed milk. I've always loved chocolate, even when I was a little kid. Most people, when they come here, they get chocolate with condensed milk. I love trying new flavors and meeting new people. It's a fun job and it's not one where you'd be embarrassed to see a friend. One thing people don't know about this stand is that we have to do all the counting in our heads. We keep it old school here, just cash no credit cards. To make the flavors, you take your extract and put four ounces of it to a gallon and you fill the rest of it with melted down sugar.

–BLaKe RaFiDi

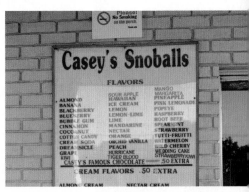

**MY THOUGHTS:** I'm not typically a stuffed snowball girl, but that's all I get when I come here. Their soft serve is actually good and is something I'd eat for pleasure, so it can only make my good snowball even better.

# Chilly's
## Snoballs

3940 Veterans Blvd., Metairie
(504) 407-3597
www.facebook.com/chillys

**My order:** Barbie with whipped cream

**Details about stand:** There's lots of seating that's uncovered, but guests can quickly retreat to under the stand's awning for shelter. They have lots of flavors, including hard-to-find ones like hazelnut, cajun red hot, dill pickle, and golden apple. Tamales, hot dogs, chips, nachos, and chip pies (Fritos, Doritos, Cheetos) are sold here. Most importantly, there's a drive-through.

> My favorite flavor is wedding cake, and since I work at a stand I get to try all the flavors—and it never gets to be too much. I liked bubble gum a lot when I was a kid. My favorite thing about working at the stand is eating everything here! The hardest thing about working at a snowball stand is knowing just how much sugar you're consuming, the fifty pounds of sugar that go into the bucket. A lot of families come through our drive-through, and we get a lot of orders in each car. When I was a little kid I remember going to Ro-Bear's in Harahan.

–Michelle LaFrance

**MY THOUGHTS:** I love when snowball stands have chocolate soft serve for stuffed snowballs, because I'm really not a vanilla girl. There are so many ice cream toppings too, which go great on snowballs. However, I've got to remember to only use the drive through when it's not busy on Vets, because trying to pull out during rush hour was a stressful task. Thankfully though, I had a snowball to ease my nerves!

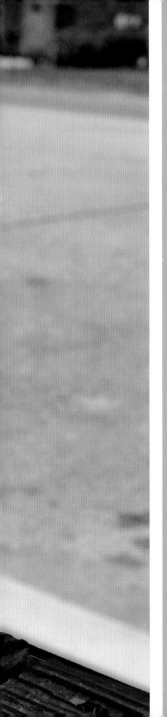

# COLD SPOT

## 2837 Barataria Blvd., Marrero
## (504) 349-3444

**MY ORDER:** Pineapple upside down cake

**DETAILS ABOUT STAND:** There's a covered area to stand and eat snowballs, and their flavor list includes a lot of the kiddie flavors, like Smurf, Pokemon, Ninja Turtle, and Spongebob. They also sell ice cream treats.

> Today I have the mystery flavor at the Cold Spot here in beautiful Marrero, Louisiana. And they told me what it was, and it's really good. A combination of their Polar Punch and lemonade. It's a beautiful blue color, and I think the ice is really good. Only $1.25, it's a nice treat, and it's not too sweet. You can really taste the flavor.
>
> I get a snowball every three or four years, but my favorite is the Satsuma at Hansen's. It's one of the best ones I've ever had. Growing up in Arkansas, we didn't have snowballs. So I didn't know about them 'til I came to New Orleans as an adult. When I had my first snowball, I was appalled at how sweet it was. That's why I only eat one every three years. And I love the chocolate one at Jazz Fest!

— JUDY WALKER

**MY THOUGHTS:** The employees were friendly, and my snowball was good. Seems like a nice place if you're in the area especially. I had trouble finding it with GPS though, and wonder if they'd consider getting one of those banners that drivers can see easily.

# Dino's
## sno-balls & ice cream

4524 S. I-10 Service Road W., Metairie
(504) 261-1198

My Order: Wild cherry with condensed milk

Details about stand: You can either drive through or walk up to this little snowball stand on the service road. In addition to snowballs, there are ice cream goodies, Italian ice, smoothies, and typical snowball stand snacks. They also sometimes sell jambalaya.

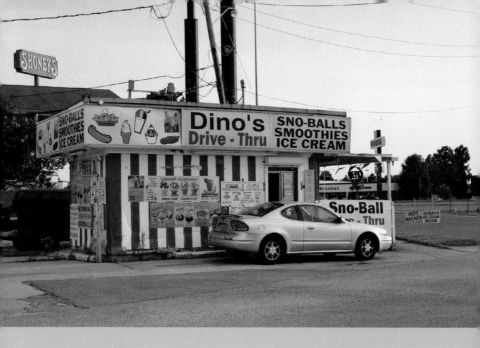

**MY THOUGHTS:** I need to try coming here after a hectic Metairie errand running day. The service is always friendly, and the snowballs are just what you'd imagine.

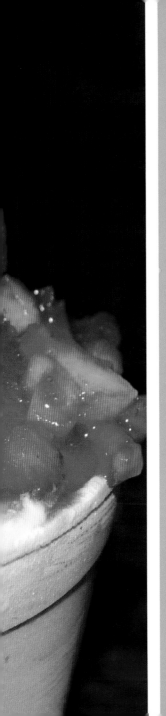

# Fat City

## Snoballs

3613 18th St., Metairie
(504) 214-6205
www.facebook.com/fatcitysnoballs

**My order:** Extreme strawberry lemonade

**Details about stand:** It's indoors with a good bit of seating and a little parking. The menu is full of specialty snowballs.

*Closed as of fall 2016

> I've been working in snowballs for about three years, and my favorite snowball to make is granny smith apple. I like sour tangy stuff. For the sweet stuff, I like watermelon. I like to keep it simple. Bubble gum when I was a kid, definitely. Working at SnoWizard I got to start trying a lot of different flavors, and I really loved a few of them. We have a huge Latino customer fan base, and they often order our mango, guava, piña colada, and watermelon.

–Melissa Bourgeois

**MY THOUGHTS:** The extreme strawberry lemonade was great and there are a few other treats I'm eager to try.

# Flavors
## Snoballs

500 Vintage Dr., Kenner
(504) 475-1211
www.facebook.com/flavorssnoballs

**My order:** Ghirardelli chocolate with condensed milk

**Details about stand:** The attention to detail is phenomenal: WiFi, outlet covers to protect babies, high chairs, mosaic tile counter, snowball decor, paper towels on each table. Snowballs, ice cream treats, and traditional snowball stand snacks are served.

> My wife is getting sour apple and sour watermelon. These are more my wife's thing, honestly. I get them for her. As a kid I used to eat them a lot, and I always got bubble gum from a stand off of Claiborne. We come to this stand a lot because we live right down the street. I remember always getting snowballs on hot days, but I'm just not really into too much sweet now.

– Jarnell Demesme

**MY THOUGHTS:** This was the best chocolate snowball I've ever had. Visiting the stands, at least three told me their specialty was chocolate. I'd get a sample and be underwhelmed usually. But this chocolate is creamy and tastes like success and diamonds and pearls! It's like sending a "Do you like me? Check yes, no, or maybe" note to your crush and he scratches out all the boxes and writes, "Will you marry me?" instead. I want to go back and chill, as Flavors has a great vibe, but I'm just going to always get the same flavor.

# THE FRIGID ZONE
## SNO-BALLS

### 2201 Lapalco Blvd., Harvey
### (504) 491-5430

**MY ORDER:** Butterbeer

**DETAILS ABOUT STAND:** Housed in a truck in a strip mall parking lot, this stand still has seating, a great selection of flavors, ice cream treats with all the toppings, and a detailed menu of kiddie flavors. No more asking about each different kiddie flavor to satisfy your picky kid. The best part is that there's a pupuseria in the strip mall, so this is the perfect place for dessert.

> I've got cantaloupe with condensed milk, and that's what I've been getting for about two and a half years. When I was a little kid, I used to get banana and cantaloupe. I'm always here because I'm a lifeguard nearby, but I used to go to the one on Gretna Boulevard before it got demolished. I used to go there every day at 1 o'clock after the girls at Blenk got out of school. My grandpa used to take me every day I was at the house in the summer.
>
> –jordan ortega

**MY THOUGHTS:** I love that even though this stand is so small, it's got so much to offer. I also love how Jordan talked about wanting to go see the girls after school, because that's one of the most fun parts of visiting snowball stands for high school kids. That will never change.

# Galvez Goodies

2036 Caffin Ave., New Orleans
(504) 319-8855
www.facebook.com/ggoodies14

**MY Order:** Daiquiri snowball

**DeTaiLS aBOUT STanD:** This stand is inside of a corner store, so the possibilities are endless as far as what to buy to go with your snowball: fried chicken, donuts, turkey necks. There's covered seating outside, and you pay inside and are served outside.

> I come to this snowball stand all the time, and I usually get wedding cake and ice cream. I think when I was a kid, I started off with strawberry and the other basic stuff. That's the only thing I ever remember getting besides wedding cake. The snowball stand I went to growing up was a little mom and pop like in the back of somebody's house—you know how we do it. It's a really cool treat, especially on extremely hot days.
>
> –KRISTOL SMITH

**MY THOUGHTS:** This stand makes me smile because it's in the first grocery to open in the Lower 9th Ward since Katrina, thanks to Burnell and Keasha Colton. I love supporting such a forward-thinking couple and am eager to watch their success.

# goody's
## sno-balls

2229 Palmisano Blvd., Chalmette
www.facebook.com/goodyssnoballs

**MY Order:** Cherry cheesecake with whipped cream and a cherry on top

**DETAILS ABOUT STAND:** Behind the Chalmette High stadium, this snowball stand has outdoor seating—some covered and some open—and several snowball flavors available. There's also candy, chips, and nachos. They are famous for their chocolate flavor.

> I always get chocolate, even when I was a kid. I get it stuffed with vanilla ice cream and topped with condensed milk. I've been coming to Goody's since I was a kid. It was just everyday life. My dad always took us to get them, and he always got ice cream.

–Neal Sartalamacchia

**MY THOUGHTS:** Whenever I'm in St. Bernard Parish—which is very often—I'm either on Judge Perez, St. Bernard Highway, or Paris Road. So I'd never seen Goody's, but I'd heard people mention it. I was delighted with the service and with the snowball, so I'll be back sooner than later.

# Hansen's
## Sno-Bliz

4801 Tchoupitoulas St., New Orleans
(504) 891-9788
www.snobliz.com

**My order:** Atomic watermelon: watermelon snowball topped with cream, crushed pineapple, marshmallow fluff, ice cream, and a cherry

**Details about stand:** There's almost always a line extending out the door and past the building, but it's worth it. Inside is full of articles and photos that tell the Hansen's story. All flavors and toppings are made at the store, with several seasonal specials. Snowballs and ice cream are their thing, so this isn't where you'll find nachos or pickles.

My favorite stand growing up was Rodney's because that was all we had in New Orleans East. As I got older, I experimented with other places. So I do enjoy Pandora and the one by Brother Martin now. We don't go there often now since they moved to the bigger building, so I would say Rodney's and Pandora's are where I go now usually.

My dad would take me to get your basic snowballs. Tutti frutti was my mom's flavor; mine was either kiwi, spearmint, wild cherry, every once in a while I would get tutti frutti but that was more for my mother. So we would just go as a family to get our snowballs and that was it, you know. My dad always got condensed milk on his, where I don't. I don't like any type of topping or anything of that nature on my snowball. I just want a plain snowball.

My favorite memory now is today because I've never been to Hansen's and I was busy in line reading an article from the *Times-Picayune* about the Hansen family and about how Ashley runs it now, and when I walked over to the other counter and looked up she was staring right at me. I looked back down at the article and her picture's in there, and I looked back up at her like oh my goodness! I'm reading an article about you as I'm standing in front of you. . . . I didn't know what to expect, I told her I didn't think she'd be here. She goes, "Oh no, I'm here every day."

–Erin Johnson

**MY THOUGHTS:** Admittedly, it took about three visits to Hansen's before I really got the hype. When you've never been there before, and aren't used to a place that believes "there are no shortcuts to quality," you get impatient waiting. But I'm a huge fan now, especially during the off-season events, like the Christmas snowball specials! They really make divine snowballs, perfectly flavored with no ice chunks.

# ike's

## snowballs

520 City Park Ave., New Orleans
(504) 208-9983
www.ikessnowballs.com

**MY order:** Cucumber melon

**DETAILS ABOUT STAND:** Right across from Delgado, this stand has all the traditional flavors and a few fun ones, like ruby pomegranate and cucumber melon. They also have snowballs for pets, boudin, nachos, hot dogs, and other traditional snowball stand fare. The seating is perfect and ample.

> I always get coconut now, but when I was a kid I only liked the ice cream flavor. In high school is when I started to like the coconut flavor, so ever since then it's been coconut. I grew up in the French Quarter, where we didn't have too many snowball stands at all. So there was one when I was in high school, by the Royal Street Pharmacy. They had a side window with a snowball stand. But I used to just drive Uptown and go to Plum Street, that was my favorite.
>
> I went to a camp called Jimmy Club in St. Rose, so we would bus there every day and bus home. It was run by the Coleman family, and it's still there. My daughter has been there too. But every day before you got back on the bus to go home, you got a snowball. It was pretty cool. They had a stand practically on the grounds of the camp, and they had just one flavor every day, like spearmint or ice cream. It was the perfect thing to do before you got back on a hot bus.

–Nina English

**MY THOUGHTS:** This is my favorite snowball stand because it's consistently good. Whenever friends want to grab a quick snowball, I insist we go here. There are sour flavors, creamy flavors, fruity flavors, nachos, boudin, and so many toppings! Service is great and so are the prices.

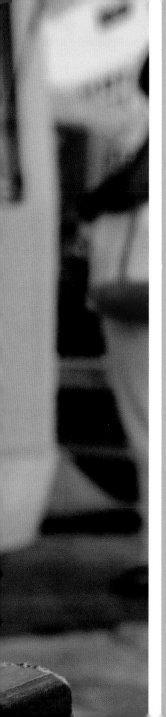

# IMPERIAL
## WOODPECKER SNO-BALLS

1 Poydras St., Riverwalk's Spanish Plaza,
& 3511 Magazine St., New Orleans
(504) 264-7170
www.iwsnoballs.com

**MY ORDER:** Pink grapefruit with condensed milk

**DETAILS ABOUT STAND:** A little truck in Spanish Plaza with delightful flavors including tamarind, lychee, and cardamom—and expertly shaved ice. Just snowballs and Zapp's, no extras.

> My husband is from New Orleans, so we come every couple years. Piña colada. This is the first time having a New Orleans snowball. All they had when I was a kid was grape and strawberry and orange. That was it. This was in Oklahoma. In Seattle we have snow cones, and we don't have all these flavors.
>
> —Patricia Moses

**MY THOUGHTS:** I first wrote about Imperial Woodpecker when it was in New York, and I heard about it while at Hansen's for the first time. Fred Axelrod, a former Hansen's employee, was in line showing his son photos of his days working there. He mentioned to me that while in New York, he had met a New Orleans girl, Neesa Peterson, who'd opened a stand there that was comparable to Hansen's. They sure are, and the "grown-up" ones she serves at galas are divine.

# Lickety Split's
## Sweet Shop

1043 Poland Ave., New Orleans
(504) 500-7669
www.facebook.com/licketysplitsnola

**My order:** Calliope Pop

**Details about stand:** There's fun '50s malt shop, bowling alley, skating rink decor, as well as a wheelchair ramp and library at this indoor stand serving solely snowballs.

> Chocolate with condensed milk was always my favorite, but as I test the waters more often I'm getting into Tiger's Blood, blue raspberry, and pear, as well. We have a lot of people who come who aren't from here and don't know what to get. So they ask me what's good, and of course they always ask what Tiger's Blood or the Calliope Pop is. Sometimes they want something with a New Orleans twist, like a Hurricane. The nectar is a New Orleans favorite. Pomegranate is something new we decided to try out, since we wanted to offer a lot of non-traditional flavors that people didn't have. Blue raspberry is one that's hard to find, [and] cantaloupe.
>
> I think a lot of people don't understand what science there is to snowball making. Basically what it comes down to is how fine is your ice. Especially in New Orleans because if you want a New Orleans-style snowball, you want it to be easy to eat where it melts in your mouth. There's certain things you can do to make a better shave. First of all you want your blades to be super, super sharp. The way that you pull when you're cranking to shave the ice, you don't want to crank too hard and get your shave too thick. And you want your ice to be super, super cold too because once your ice blocks start to get even a bit melty, that's when the ice starts bonding before it even hits the cup and that's when you start to get those little chunks. There actually is a science to snowball making and it's not as easy as it looks, but it can be when you do everything you're supposed to do.
>
> —PAULETTE CALLAHAN

**MY THOUGHTS:** In 1996/1997, "Project Pops" or "Calliope Pops" became de rigueur for us "hood kids." They were these delicious suckers called watermelon slice pops, and I remember getting tons from Joe's Package Liquor on St. Bernard to lure my then crush, Brent Balthazar. They were sweet, creamy, and tangy, and I can still see myself pulling a roll out of a brown paper bag. Even as an adult, I feel like somebody when I have them. My advice is to check Facebook before visiting this stand, because the hours are a bit loose.

# Lou-Lou's
## snoballs & ice cream

734 Papworth Ave., Metairie
(504) 400-2446

**MY ORDER:** Candy apple with caramel

**DETAILS ABOUT STAND:** The ice is perfectly smooth and there's a wide variety of flavors, including seasonal ones and quite a few natural ones. Ice cream treats and traditional snowball stand snacks are also sold. There's a covered picnic table and patio for seating.

> I've only been here for a few months, but my friend now owns it and has been working here for ten years. They actually split up the two Lou-Lou's. They're still friendly, they just aren't affiliated like they were.
>
> We try to stay on top of keeping the ice soft, even though it's a really hard thing to accomplish. We actually get ice delivered as well as making our own ice here. Our natural snowballs, we put very little sweetener in it. We used to only have the natural strawberry, but now we've branched out and offer blueberry, watermelon, lemonade, mango-pineapple.

> When I was a kid I loved bubble gum. . . . But here, I love our chocolate cream and white chocolate macadamia nut. Anytime I don't know what I want, chocolate it is. I also love our natural watermelon and natural strawberry. And I like condensed milk on the bottom and the top, that way you can reach down to the bottom because I don't like when it gets eaten up by the ice. A lot of people use the pet milk or the sugar-free instead of the condensed milk.
>
> Before I was born, my mom and dad actually owned a snowball stand. Working here has been great because I've loved snowballs all my life. And I was already a bartender and into that mixology. So this was a very easy switch over because now I'm just a non-alcoholic bartender.

–Yvonne Rearick

**MY THOUGHTS:** When I was pregnant, I would come here just for the ice. It's so smooth, with nary a chunk. Fine powder. My friend chef Adam Superneau of Oak Oven told me about this place, so that's when I tried it. All the flavors are really great, especially the natural flavors.

# Mom & Pop
## Snowballs and Hot Tamales

### 7479 St. Claude Ave., Arabi

**My order:** Malted milk snowball and chili cheese fries

**Details about stand:** There's ample parking here and there's seating with an umbrella for shade. I'd never seen a malted milk snowball before coming here. Their snowball flavor selection also includes such rare flavors as pumpkin pie, peanut butter, and cherry cola. The snack selection is extensive, including tamales, gumbo, and burgers; and they use seasoned fries instead of plain shoestring potatoes.

My favorite snowball flavor is the sour apple because even when you get it sugar-free, it's the best ever. And for regular flavors, my favorite would be the Pink Lady [or] grasshopper. I've always liked the Pink Lady, even when I was a kid. My parents used to have a snowball stand back when I was little, and that was one of the main flavors. It was right there on Saint Claude, Alfonso's Snowballs at Alfonso's Shell station. You gotta have that soft ice, service with a smile, and always treat your customers right—when you give them food, give them a lot! Just like Rocky and Carlos, even the child's plate is overflowing. We try to do that. Quality food is the most important.

–Nina Daughtry

**MY THOUGHTS:** These were the best chili cheese fries I've had in my life, and there was a time in high school when I'd eat chili cheese fries almost any time I saw them on a menu. The people were so friendly too, so I'm looking forward to returning soon to try many more things.

# Mr. Frank's
## snoballs

2215 Hickory Ave., Harahan
(504) 484-1640
www.facebook.com/mrfrankssnoballs

**My order:** Natural watermelon

**Details about stand:** The flavor list is short, but it includes natural snowballs with no artificial colors or flavors. They sell nachos and ice cream as well, and they accept credit cards.

> I come to Mr. Frank's often, since it's in my neighborhood. I got the wild cherry for my daughter and the wedding cake for me. I've only been getting wedding cake for the last two years. When I was a child I always had grape, but as I matured I got into nectar and a lot of other different kinds. But I like wedding cake because it doesn't stain and it won't be in your teeth.
>
> I don't remember much about when I would get snowballs when I was a kid, but I remember taking my kids and them being just covered in their first snowballs, the grape and bubble gum.
>
> —Mary Oestriecher

OPEN

BUSINESS HOURS
MON 12:00 TO 9:00
TUE 12:00 TO 9:00
WED 12:00 TO 9:00
THU 12:00 TO 9:00
FRI 12:00 TO 9:00
SAT 12:00 TO 9

**MY THOUGHTS:** I love being able to get natural snowballs, because I really don't like diet things, but I know I shouldn't go crazy with sugar all the time. I also think this would be the perfect place to continue a movie date.

# NOLA SNOW

908 Harrison Ave.
& 7040 Vicksburg St., New Orleans
(504) 373-6555
www.nolasnow.com

**MY ORDER:** Chocolate with condensed milk

**DETAILS ABOUT STAND:** A consistent stand in Lakeview with covered seating. Not many flavors, but there are two flavors of soft serve for stuffing snowballs. They also sell nachos and ice cream treats.

I work at NOLA Beans, so I come here all the time after work. I really do love this snowball stand. I really love Pink Princess, which is one of their signature flavors, and I get it with sour apple. So that's really, really good. Those are great together. But today I tried coconut and Hawaiian, so I'm trying something different. For my mom, I get half blueberry half ice cream and then she stuffs it with soft serve vanilla ice cream. The only thing about blueberry and blue flavors is that it stains your mouth and you can't, like, have blue teeth. The kids love it, but you can't go to work with blue teeth.

When I was little, I really liked strawberry and pineapple, or I would get bubble gum and ice cream. You know, kiddie flavors. And I would get soft serve ice cream on top. My mom used to take us every day after summer camp on the lakefront at UNO. And we used to go to the one on Elysian Fields right by Brother Martin. A couple of times, you know of course, I dropped it and I was hysterical about it, but my mom got me another one to calm me down.

–Sarah Pannia

**MY THOUGHTS:** I have a very foggy memory of going here when I was a kid and my Paw Paw worked at Delgado. I don't get to come here much, but I've got cousins in Lakeview who come often and really enjoy it. It's a Lakeview institution for sure.

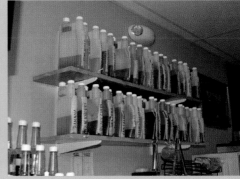

# The Original
## New Orleans
## Snoball & Smoothie

4339 Elysian Fields Ave., New Orleans
(504) 283-8370

**My order:** Strawberry shortcake with strawberries and whipped cream

**Details about stand:** The "green house by Brother Martin" has been an institution in Gentilly for at least twenty years and is one of very few stands open year round. They sell snowballs, smoothies, ice cream, nachos, Frito pies, po'boys, and just about everything really. There's a covered outdoor patio, and the stand itself is indoors.

"

My favorite snowball flavor right now is Tiger's Blood. When I was a kid, it was probably something basic like a strawberry, bubble gum. Something like that. This was actually my first job, and I started when I was fifteen, worked until I was seventeen. And then I quit but I came back about two years ago. So I've been here for a while. Since we moved next door, we brought out a lot more food. It gets crazy sometimes in the day. I know sometimes you pass by and the line is out the door.

As for ordering tips, getting sizes first is a big plus. If we get the sizes first, we'll come back for the flavors. You get your regular customers everyday, the ones where you see them coming and you make their snowball whenever you see them pull up. They come every day and it's nice.

−Kerry Disalvo

"

**MY THOUGHTS:** I've got so many memories of this stand. Sitting with my mom while she caught up with her friends, going here with my friends for my birthday, tripping on a tree trunk and falling in front of the cute Brother Martin boys when I was in high school, laughing at my best friend Erica for wanting a flavor that matched her outfit. And they still have some of the best snowball stand nachos in the city.

# PANDORA'S
## SNOWBALLS

901 N. Carrollton Ave., New Orleans
(504) 486-8644
www.facebook.com/pandorassnowballs

**MY ORDER:** Sky blue cream with condensed milk

**DETAILS ABOUT STAND:** It's just enough of what you need to get in and get out when there's not a line during the after-school rush. An order window, a pickup window (both covered), and your everyday treats, plus brownie sundaes, soft serve, corn dogs, tamales, hot dogs, and nachos.

> I just get a different flavor every time, but today I got sour watermelon and pink lemonade. This is the only snowball stand I go to. When I was a kid, I was into condensed milk on anything. Stuck on strawberry and spearmint.
>
> —SHAWN TENNESSEE

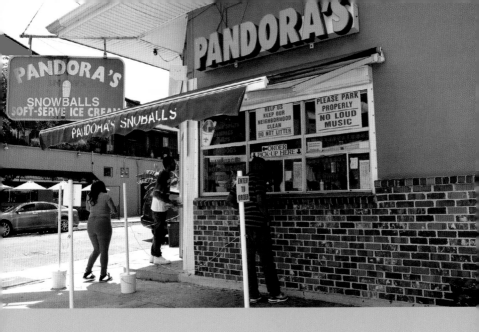

**MY THOUGHTS:** When I think of Pandora's, I think of days when my mom would pick me up from Lusher Extension, instead of catching the streetcar and Carrollton bus. She was Tiger's Blood, I was vanilla cream and ice cream with condensed milk, and my Paw Paw was pineapple.

# Piety Street
## Sno-Balls

612 Piety St., New Orleans
(504) 782-2569

- - - - - - - - - - - - - - - - - - - - - - - - - -

**My Order:** Mandarin ginger with candied ginger

**Details About Stand:** Right across from Pizza Delicious, next to Crescent Park, this stand has about as many artisanal flavors as traditional, and even has some for dogs. The snowball trashcan is adorable, as is the '50s atomic design scheme.

*Closed as of fall 2016

I normally get ice cream, but when I was a little kid I used to get strawberry from Plum Street. Just red, anything red. I've got pictures of me with my first snowball, and I'm like covered from head to toe, wearing this giant applique outfit with "Megan" and a big strawberry on it. My mom to this day loves that picture.

I used to lifeguard at a place on the Northshore that had a little stand. And as a lifeguard, we were allowed as many drinks as we wanted, and they counted snowballs as a drink. So I used to go behind the counter and make myself snowballs. Out of all the flavors they had, which were pretty gross, the only good one was ice cream. So I learned to love ice cream flavor snowballs. Since then, I've only eaten ice cream flavor snowballs. I used to get ice cream and half cotton candy, but then I was like you know what? I'm a purist.

–Megan Stryker

**MY THOUGHTS:** It took me a long time to like this stand. I was working on a feature for *Gambit* about affordable treats in the summer, and there was a guy at the stand who was a real jerk to me. Just awful! So when I was writing this book, I told my girl I wasn't going to include Piety Street because the guy was so mean and I thought the snowball was subpar. But she told me he wasn't there anymore, so I headed over. The owners were there and were so nice and the snowballs were fantastic. Great post-Pizza D treat.

# PLUM STREET
## snoballs

1300 Burdette St., New Orleans
(504) 866-7996
www.plumstreetsnoball.com

**MY Order:** Bananas Foster cream with condensed milk

**DETAILS ABOUT STAND:** It's a tiny place, but that adds to the charm. There's lots of seating outside. They only sell snowballs—no ice cream, no snacks. Snowballs. Toppings. Delicious Uptown tradition. One cool thing is that they sell freezer size snowballs.

> I got frozen mint today, but I like to switch it up. When I was a kid, I was strictly spearmint and chocolate. My boyfriend and I just stopped by today because we were in the neighborhood. He got orchid cream vanilla today. Nobody else knows what a snowball is except for if you live down here. Everybody else calls it snow cones and that's not a snowball.
>
> —CANDY LABICHE

**MY THOUGHTS:** In those good ol' Lusher Extension days, we'd all come here and get snowballs. Mostly to be cute. I'd always get the pail and get juice all over me, and it wasn't until I was an adult that an Uptown friend told me they sold plastic bags to cover your pails. The flavors here are always awesome, and the snow is just thick enough to have some bulk. One day, I'm getting the Rocket '88.

# PONTILLY SNO

3968 Old Gentilly Road, New Orleans
(504) 303-8173
www.facebook.com/pontillysno

**MY Order:** Nachos with cheese and peppers and a Snow Angel snowball with condensed milk

**DETAILS ABOUT STAND:** Pontilly Sno is open year round and there's seating indoors and outside, including high chairs and booster seats. It's part of the Bethel Community Baptist Church, so there's Christian music playing and there are Bible scriptures painted on walls. One of the best things is the variety of soft serve for stuffing snowballs, including piña colada, butter pecan, and caramel flavors.

> There was a snowball stand near my house. I stay off Hayne, and it was called Snow Blizzard. It was next to a school. And I just remember being young and just in the summer, taking trips down there with my dad especially—when my dad was still alive. So I connect getting snowballs with him. I just associate summer with snowballs. Especially being from here, from New Orleans. I definitely matured with my flavors as I got older. I used to get rainbow or sour apple, but now I get strawberry cream and nectar cream and get it stuffed. Tips aren't required but are always appreciated. I say anything between $1 and $2 is a good tip because employees often split them.

—TIMOTHY LONDON

**MY THOUGHTS:** I often wonder why more snowball stands don't pony up the extra money to turn their shacks into actual lounges such as this. Not everyone is a coffee person, and I'm sure I'm not the only one who could probably tackle finals or some other big project hopped up on snowballs and nachos. As the employees promised, my Snow Angel snowball tasted like "a mouthful of Skittles."

NOW SERVING!

| | |
|---|---|
| 1 | BUTTER PECAN |
| 2 | WATERMELON |
| 3 | STRAWBERRY |
| 4 | BLUE GOO™ |
| 5 | CARAMEL |
| 6 | PINA COLADA |
| 7 | BANANA RIPPLE |
| 8 | CHOCOLATE SWIRL |

# Red Rooster
## Snowballs

2801 Washington Ave., New Orleans
(504) 895-6786
www.redroosternola.com

**My Order:** Piña colada with condensed milk and yakamein

**Details about Stand:** It's a bright red stand with well-distanced order and pickup windows, and a whole lot of covered seating. There are just enough snowball flavors, but the food menu is likely the most extensive I've seen at a snowball stand, with yakamein, fish plates, stuffed peppers, crawfish nachos, po'boys, and more.

Candy apple is my favorite flavor and this is the first place I ever saw it. I used to be a wedding cake guy. I occasionally get toppings on my snowballs, and when I do it's usually condensed milk. If I'm at Hansen's, they put love into theirs, and I usually get the strawberry topping. When I was a kid we used to joke about me getting either red or blue. We didn't even know what the flavors were, we just did it by color. It was like red, blue, or rainbow, that's how we used to order them. We used to go to Casey's on the Westbank, on Behrman right by French Riviera Fitness. They may have changed names by now. And there's another over by General Meyer by the Chubbie's—Van's! That's the one I went to the most as a kid. I had snowballs so much, because it's so hot in New Orleans. So it makes sense that Hansen's motto is "Air-Condition Your Tummy," because I think that's what kids did.

I remember most of the bad experiences, like getting a snow cone at the Ringling Brothers and Barnum and Bailey Circus. And I remember how awful it was, like "Why is it so hard? Why is everything on the bottom?" Those are the things that as a kid I remember, like being really upset. And that's when I first learned the difference between a snow cone and a snowball.

—Lui Caleon

**MY THOUGHTS:** I'd heard whispers in the 'hood about this place for a while, but I'm a 7th Ward girl so I'm not much for Uptown. But it was good and the service was friendly. And I was even able to find nearby parking, which I worry about Uptown.

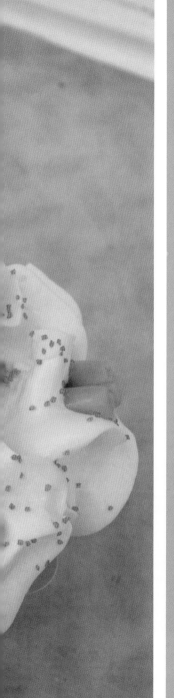

# River Breez
## Sno Balls

4800 E. Saint Bernard Hwy., New Orleans
(504) 610-1679
www.riverbreezsnoballs.com

**My order:** Hello Kitty (cotton candy, toasted marshmallow, stuffed with whipped cream, and sprinkles)

**Details about stand:** Located on the highway in the front of a house, this stand has an entire menu of specialty flavors with fun toppings. There's a little bench for seating, and credit cards are accepted.

> I come here often, and I try to get something different each time I come. It's me, my two kids, my mom, my dad, my husband, my brother—all of us come here now. Today I'm just getting the nachos and cheese, but my little girl and them, they do the stuffed snow-balls. They are really big and full here, and she always puts the gummy bears and stuff. I was a chocolate and condensed milk as a kid, and then I went to cookies and cream with condensed milk. That's what I tell my kids, don't get the regular stuff and get some-thing that's gonna give you some kind of taste. When we were lit-tle, my mom used to take everybody to go get them. But now that everybody grew up, on the weekends we all get to her house and come here. I used to go to Sugar Shack because they put the most juice in the snowballs.
>
> —Brittany Walker

NACHO's w/CHEESE/Peppers $3.50
EXTRA CHEESE or PEPPERS $.50 ea.
CHIPS $1.00 PICKLES $1.00
CHIPS-N-CHEESE $2.00
BOTTLE WATER $1.00
NEW FLAVORS
BLACK CHERRY   ROOT BEER

**MY THOUGHTS:** When I go to a snowball stand, I often have trouble picking a flavor combination and the toppings to go with it. At this stand, that work is already done for me. There are so many specialty snowballs I want to try here.

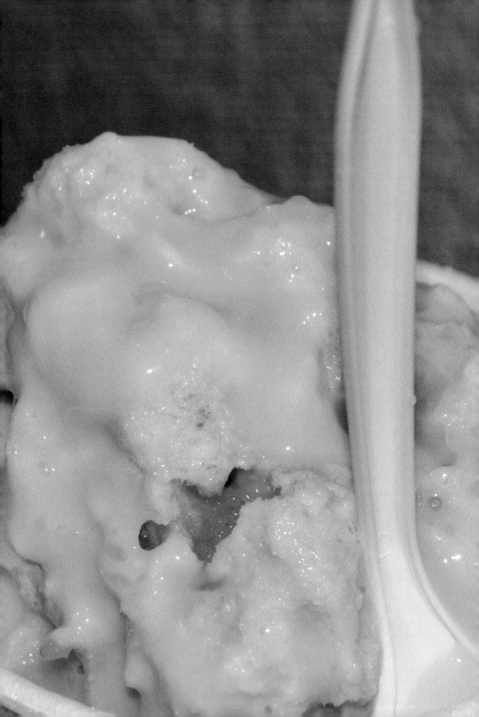

# Ro-Bear's

## 6969 Jefferson Hwy., Harahan
## (504) 737-5013

**My Order:** Blue Hawaii

**Details About Stand:** A Harahan favorite for years, this stand serves snowballs and ice cream treats. At night there's always a crowd, but it moves quickly. The neon signs are wonderful to gaze upon in the evening, and the sunsets are always gorgeous near the stand.

Tonight I'm just getting a soft serve cup for now, a soft serve swirl cone for my landlord, and a spearmint snowball for later. I just put it in the freezer to keep it. I really have this inclination to try all these different kinds, but I just can't get away from spearmint and nectar. Spearmint was my daddy's flavor and nectar was my mama's flavor, so I feel like something's there with that. Like it's in the blood. I wanna get all these other ones! I wanna get yellow cake; I wanna get some almond wedding cake. But . . . it's just so hard to break away from spearmint. We grew up in Old Algiers and went to one on General Meyer way down. If I get dreamsicle, I'll get condensed milk on top.

— Jami ROSS

RO-BEAR'S
SNO-BALLS
SOFT SERVE ICE CREAM

**MY THOUGHTS:** My friend Bridget Gillane took me here once, and I loved it! It's one of the stands she was raised on, along with Casey's and Sal's. When I was pregnant, I'd come out here and get two snowballs: blue Hawaii and orchid cream vanilla.

# RODNEY'S

9231 Lake Forest Blvd., New Orleans
(504) 241-2035

**MY ORDER:** Cotton candy cream

**DETAILS ABOUT STAND:** This is a landmark New Orleans East snowball stand, so there's almost always a line. It moves quickly though, and they are open year round. Rodney's is famous for putting gummy bears in their snowballs, and they have a pretty extensive food menu with sundaes, nachos, shakes, tamales, and more. Their ice is some of the best in the city, and their flavors taste exactly like they should.

> Ice cream and cream is my favorite everywhere. I just like the creamy flavors because they're so sweet and they taste really close to what they say they're supposed to be. Like the ice cream tastes just like ice cream. Crazy thing is, when I was young I used to not like snowballs. Yes, I was THAT New Orleans kid. . . . It wasn't until college when I went to Plum Street and they had the creamy flavors that I started liking snowballs for real, for real. And then I had the nectar cream and then I had the ice cream. So I discovered the ice cream and cream at Plum Street, then I came here and they had it. I was like, "It's the best thing ever." I like the cream flavors, and I don't even get the regular ones because I just don't like the way they taste.

> And when we came here [when I was a kid], I would just make my mouth blue with the snowball and then eat the gummy bear and throw the rest away. That's all I wanted was the gummy bear and to make my mouth blue, because you'd walk around with your mouth blue and everybody would be like, "Oh you just came from the snowball stand?" and you'd be like "Yeah!" It's a conversation piece. Nachos and the snowball stand was always a thing. So since I didn't like the snowballs, we would come here, we'd get the nachos and sometimes I'd get the soft serve ice cream. I like it when the chips get just a little soggy and you gotta get them out of the cheese with your finger. And you lick out all the pepper juice. I feel like nachos and snowballs go together. It's like a combo meal when you get fast food.

—ROB CARTER III

**MY THOUGHTS:** I wasn't raised in New Orleans East, but most of my relatives and friends of the family lived here. So my family and I would be in the East every weekend usually, and even now I still find myself in the East about once a week for some reason or another. Going to Rodney's reminds me of being in high school and hoping to see the cute boys that lived in the East out at the Plaza.

# SAL'S

## SNO-BALLS

1823 Metairie Rd., Metairie
(504) 666-1823

**MY ORDER:** Cherry sip with condensed milk

**DETAILS ABOUT STAND:** Instead of chairs and tables, there are tree stumps and logs to sit on. There's a flavor for everyone here, including the elusive white chocolate and chips, and ice cream treats are also sold. Late night hours are a big draw here.

I like cherry with condensed milk. I just had to do rainbow when I was a kid. I just had to! It doesn't taste that great, but it looks cool at first. We went to the one on Harrison a lot, the one by the pet store. So we'd always go there after school and get our snowballs and look at pets and beg for animals. It's a nice after school treat. I think it's something parents love to do with kids. It can be a nice bribe.

## –Stephanie Moises

I like nectar cream with condensed milk. I used to love Batman, though I still don't really know what it is. And rainbow, even though it looks horrible once it's melted together. When I worked at a stand and tried to make rainbow, they'd always turn black. I always had to ask the other person at the stand to make it for me because I couldn't do it. It literally always turned black. I worked at a snowball stand for the summer after I graduated high school, the stand on Fleur de Lis and Harrison called Firehouse Snowballs. I had my wisdom teeth taken out that summer, and I'd go to get malts there, because they gave me free malts after I left. The most fun part was harvesting the ice.

## –Christian Moises

**MY THOUGHTS:** I was a grown woman before I'd ever tried Sal's, mostly because I was wary of going to Old Metairie. But I love Sal's so much now, especially because the tree stump seats make me feel like I'm either a little girl at a fancy sleep-away camp or Cindy Bear. My son had his first snowball here in 2015, and many agree that their spearmint is the best around.

# Scuba Steve's

## 2400 Barataria Blvd., Marrero
## (504) 341-8967

**MY ORDER:** Coconut with chocolate dip

**DETAILS ABOUT STAND:** The most exciting part of this stand is that you can get chocolate-dipped snowballs. The entire snowball, dipped in chocolate. There are also funnel cakes, ice cream treats, and brownies. There's a little table to sit and eat, but most patrons seemed to get back on the road.

Today I had wine cooler and wedding cake. I used to always get nectar with condensed milk as a kid.

### –Michael Brisco

I had the piña colada and wedding cake and liked piña colada as a kid.

### –Khalil Noah

I got the Frog in a Blender with wedding cake. My favorite as a kid was ice cream.

### –Ronald Smith

**MY THOUGHTS:** This is my other favorite snowball stand, on the strength of the chocolate dipping and friendly service. I'm still looking for the perfect chocolate-dipped snowball here, so I'm going back more often than a bit.

# SHIVERING SAM'S
## SNOWBALLS

### 30 Westbank Expy., Gretna
### (504) 398-0928

**MY ORDER:** Coconut cream

**DETAILS ABOUT STAND:** It's on the Westbank Expressway, right by Oakwood Mall. There's nowhere to sit, but there is a drive-through and there are several places to park and eat.

I just tried a caramel snowball with an orange gummy bear on top. If there's a syrup that's homemade at that particular stand, I like to try that. I also like to see what other people like. And I like the cream flavors, but not always. And I think when it's super, duper hot out, going for a big fruity flavor is always a favorite.

In Texas, where I'm from, the snowballs are more of an icy thing—like shards of ice. I think it's because they don't have the good machines, haven't invested in them like New Orleans does. It's hard, it takes a while to eat it. You have to stand outside in the Texas heat for a little bit and let it melt. So I think that's one of the reasons it's not as popular out there. Because when you're a little kid and you're trying to eat it and you're biting into it and you can't. . . . I feel like the texture is really important. The thing in Texas is Blue Bell ice cream. So if you're gonna go out for an icy treat in Texas, you're gonna get Blue Bell ice cream.

I love the snowball stand on Magazine near Louisiana because they sell snowballs, hot dogs, they have a picnic table outside. But if we're planning to go get a snowball with friends, you've gotta think about what's in the neighborhood and which places are favorites.

–sara HUDSON

**MY THOUGHTS:** I can see myself hitting this place up after a mall trip, definitely. Though there aren't many frills, it's cute and clean with tasty and affordable snowballs. A perfect place to go if you are on the Westbank and need a quick fix.

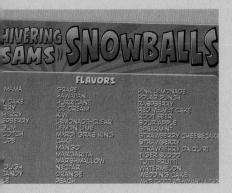

# Sno Shak

4001 Jefferson Hwy., Jefferson
(504) 304-7174

**My Order:** Mystic Blue snowball

**Details about Stand:** This is one of my favorite types of stands because there's a big area between the ordering window and the pick-up window, and because they serve ice cream with lots of toppings that you can also use on a snowball.

> Basically we come get it a lot. We were on our way to Elmwood, and my son was just like, "Ma, let's stop and get a snowball." So it's maybe three times a week, maybe? And I always get wedding cake, I never change. And he always gets blue bubblegum.

–Demetria Lawson

**MY THOUGHTS:** I remember going to this stand with my friend Christy Malbrew not long after Katrina, after we left Dillard's Hilton outpost in search of a snowball stand open Sundays. I think it's a really fine stand, with excellent ice and a wide array of delicious flavors.

# Sno-La

## Snoball Lounge

2311 N. Causeway Blvd., Metairie
& 8108 Hampson St., New Orleans
(504) 327-7669
www.sno-la.com

**My order:** Bananas Foster stuffed with cheesecake and topped with condensed milk

**Details about stand:** There are traditional flavors here, but you're doing yourself a disservice if you don't try one of their specialty cheesecake-stuffed snowballs. It's also one of the few indoor snowball stands, with a restroom, WiFi, and comfy seating.

> When I was little I liked bubble gum and childish flavors, but when I got older I liked wedding cake and ice cream. This is the fourth snowball stand I've worked at since I was sixteen. I just always ended up getting a job at a snowball stand. But this one is the best one I've been at. It's very, very professional. My favorite to make is Super Strawberry Lemonade because it's got lots of strawberries.

### –Lester Bloom

> Now that I'm sixteen it's Granny Smith, but when I was little it was Tiger's Blood. It's my first job. I love to make the Darryl's Delight because it's got the ice cream and the strawberries.

### – Josh Duhon

**MY THOUGHTS:** I remember when this stand first opened, when it was near the Beary Cherry Tree daycare. Their new location is easier to get to during high traffic times, so that's a plus. My friend Waymon Morris and I went to one of their unlimited snowball tastings, which was one of the best nights of my life. We had thirty-seven snowball samples, and I learned their peanut butter cheesecake is divine. The Beam Me Up Mikey, a peanut butter cheesecake-stuffed, condensed milk-topped, chocolate banana snowball is my favorite. However, I recommend bringing your own spoon because their spoons can be flimsy.

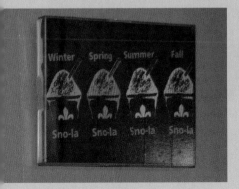

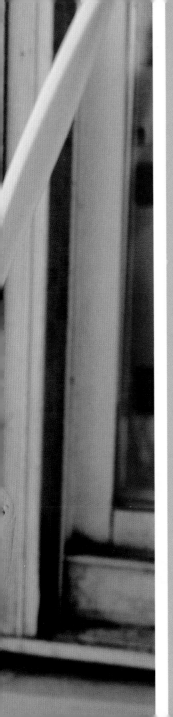

# Snow World
## Sno-Balls

629 Berhman Hwy., Terrytown
(504) 239-9365
www.facebook.com/snowworldsnoballs

**My Order:** Rocket fuel

**Details About Stand:** At this pretty pink stand, there's lots of parking and probably the best selection of sugar-free flavors. There are also ice cream treats and traditional snowball stand fare.

> I got black cherry stuffed with condensed milk on top, like I always do. When I was a kid, I just tried all the flavors. We always take my family to Snow World now that we've moved to the Westbank. But when I was a kid, it was getting a truckload of kids together from the neighborhood to go to the snowball stand. It'd be like an outing.

### –Leatrice Johnson

> Since I've been coming here for the past three days, I've been getting grape. I've been in a grape mood, but normally my one is Tiger Blood. As a kid, I always got regular strawberry or banana. I grew up and matured into the Tiger Blood, the nectar, the cream flavors. I get condensed milk usually, but not today.

### –Troy White

**MY THOUGHTS:** My best friend Elizabeth Conrad hipped me to this place one summer when we were working extra hard on getting in shape. I'd had sugar-free snowballs before and thought more than anything that the texture was awful. But these are the best sugar-free I've had. Of course, their other snowballs are yummy, too.

# SnoWizard
## Snoball Shoppe

4001 Magazine St., New Orleans
(504) 899-8758
www.snowizardsnoballshop.com

**My Order:** Melipone Mexican vanilla with condensed milk

**Details about stand:** There are shaded Adirondack chairs outside and two clean little windows for ordering and picking up. And most of the snowball stands get their flavors from here, so you can find almost any flavor: mojito, mudslide, chai latté, pectoral punch. There are also ice cream goodies and the usual snowball stand eats.

> I always get ice cream and cream, but when I was a little boy it varied. I used to work at the shoe shop down the street, so we'd come here all the time to try all the flavors. But I used to like bubble gum and strawberry—some of the more traditional flavors. I think the ice cream and cream is one of my favorites because it does the right job with the ice and makes a great combination.
>
> This is one of my favorite stands, but I love Hansen's on Tchoupitoulas. But SnoWizard, these are the folks that make the machines and the syrup and all that good stuff. This would probably be equal to the Hansen's, I just personally like the Hansen's flavors a little bit better. My two daughters love snowballs, so when they were kids I introduced them to that fine, fine ice so they would have an acquired taste. They get very judgmental about the ice and the grains and how it melts on your tongue.
>
> —Kirk Derokey

**MY THOUGHTS:** I really think it's just a perfect snowball stand. Most snowball stands in New Orleans get their flavors from here, so I think it's the best place to try a new flavor. The Melipone Mexican vanilla is so creamy and divine though, that I really have no urge to try another.

# Stop Jockin
## Sno-Ball Stand

3600 St. Bernard Ave., New Orleans
(504) 247-3221
www.facebook.com/stopjockinsnoballs/

**MY ORDER:** Key lime pie with condensed milk

**DETAILS ABOUT STAND:** This stand is attached to a barber shop, and it actually started out as a snowball truck in California. The Rockin' Berry Squeeze and Tropical Sunrise are two specialty flavors and are both outstanding. Rockin' Berry Squeeze is incredibly tart and fruity, and Tropical Sunrise tastes like something you need to drink on the beach from a hollowed coconut. Their ice is up to par with Hansen's, and they stick a gummy bear in each snowball.

> My favorite flavor is cotton candy and coconut, what I have right now. I've been getting it since . . . I remember the first time I had it. It was 2004, summertime of 2004. My best friend was working at the Grand Movie Theater in the East, and after his shift we went over to Rodney's. You know, that was our spot. I was a Rodney's baby. I grew up on the Rodney's and the snowball shop in City Park, the one across from the horse stables. And then the one in Lakeview right next to the pet shop, those were my three. But my patna' and I, we were at Rodney's. I used to be a wedding cake kinda man or ice cream, almond. And then he was like, "No, you gotta try the cotton candy mixed with the coconut" And then I was like, "Imma see what yours looks like first." And his was like this pretty, pink, clear. . . . So then I got it, and it's been my flavor ever since.

I remember always going to the one in Lakeview right next to the pet shop. No one ever knew the name, it was just the same old man that worked there. And I always remember he had the superhero flavors: the Batman, the Superman, and the Robin, or the Green Lantern. You never knew what it was, but you just got it because of the name. That was always me.

And the first time I had it stuffed was at City Park, across from the horse stable, right by Gernon Brown. That was the first time I had a scoop of ice cream at the bottom of a snowball. When you're real bad, you leave there and go to McKenzie's and get you three glazed for 89 cents. Or some buttermilk drops or some donut holes.

–Calvin Johnson Jr.

**MY THOUGHTS:** My friends Samantha Knox and Marcel Harris tried for years to get me to try this stand, but for some reason I thought a stand that close to my house couldn't possibly be good. And I was stuck on the stand I'd been going to since high school and didn't want to betray them. I'm mad at myself for taking so long. I only wish the hours were more consistent.

# Sunny's

3437 Florida Ave., Kenner
(504) 469-1842
www.facebook.com/pages/Sunnys-Snoballs/

**MY ORDER:** Raspberry

**DETAILS ABOUT STAND:** Wood paneling and black and gold letter stickers give a warm family vibe, as do the school chairs and desks. The entire operation is indoors and there's parking all around. Snowballs and ice cream treats are sold.

> I got Tiger's Blood with condensed milk today, but I usually get wedding cake or strawberry with condensed milk. I just didn't feel like getting those today. I live right down the street, so I come here often. I've been coming here since I was a kid, back when I used to get bubble gum. I don't get that anymore, or rainbow, because I think I just overdid it back then. My best friend works here, so I've been here for like three hours now. We used to go to high school together, we did our first year of college together at Southeastern, and she lives down the street from me.

–Breanna Atkins

**MY THOUGHTS:** When I got my snowball, I thought it would be dry. It looked tall and dry when I saw it, and I was sad. But once I tried it, I was transported to 1994 when I would drink all my Paw Paw's raspberry Crystal Light from the pitcher. It was just sweet enough, full of flavor, and incredibly soft.

# Sweet Shack
## Snowballs

1716 Stumpf Blvd., Gretna
www.facebook.com/Sweet-Shack-Snowballs

**MY ORDER:** Mardi Gras

**DETAILS ABOUT STAND:** Hard-to-find cherimoya is here, and they also sell ice cream goodies and standard snowball stand eats. There's a drive-through as well as picnic table seating.

> I've been working here for three years. I like wedding cake stuffed with ice cream, but as I worked in a stand I started trying different things. It's hard work because you're always on your feet, but it's fun because you make new friends. We have to lift up to fifty pounds of sugar a day, and it gets really busy with this drive-through.
>
> —Tiffany Thibodeaux

> This is my first year here. Cotton candy, Mardi Gras, and king cake are my favorites. Everyone likes snowballs, so it's nice to give people what they want. It's a lot of work, a lot of time. I don't think people know how much work goes into making your snowball.
>
> —Jenna Breaux

**MY THOUGHTS:** The girls were friendly and my snowball was nice, so I'd return but only in the drive-through. It hard, to me anyway, to park here and back up and all that.

# TAFT PARK
## SNOBALLS

### 3310 Taft Park, Metairie
### (504) 455-5517

**MY ORDER:** Apple pie à la mode

**DETAILS ABOUT STAND:** There are so many excellent specialty snowballs here, including one dedicated to the 610 Stompers. There's adorable snowball decor all around, and there's ice cream and "pup cups" for dogs.

My son Hunter worked at a CYO for four years running a snowball stand, and he decided it'd be a good idea to do one. My dad owns a barber shop, so my son decided to talk to his grandfather about opening a spot right here next to it.

### –Ronnie Cheramie

I chose to do the Facebook and all the fancy flavors and the garnishes because I feel like snowballs are fun and they should be about the kids. And once I started with the kid flavors, I sat around and started thinking about what can I do now. We both grew up in Metairie, and we always went to Casey's or the one in Schwegmann's where the Lowe's is now.

When I was a kid I used to always eat the watermelon or cotton candy. Those were my favorites. I'm a chocolate eater now with condensed milk. Peanut butter sauce tastes so good on the grape. My mom loved snowballs and even still she comes here today to critique and let us know what we're doing right, what we're not doing right.

### –Laura Cheramie

**MY THOUGHTS:** I'm the type of girl who loves craft cocktails with lots of fun garnishes and ingredients, like the ones at Cafe B or Victory. The snowballs here give me that same excited feeling, and the owners are really sweet. It'd be fun if they were open for Thanksgiving and could make a cranberry-dressing-turkey gravy thing. At least I think so.

# TASTE THIS!
## SNOWBALLS

5335 Venus St., New Orleans
(504) 943-8383

**MY ORDER:** Tangerine snowball and hot sausage on bun with cheese

**DETAILS ABOUT STAND:** There are a few benches and an umbrella at this stand, and there's a lot of food here, including yakamein and fish plates.

> There was this place called Sno Ball King in Chalmette, and it was right across from Andrew Jackson High School. And I think it was just a snowball stand in somebody's converted kitchen or garage or whatever. And the house, Katrina got that. I remember being in high school or middle school and constantly people would take the "S" from the sign so it would say No Ball King. I liked ice cream and chocolate. I always liked the cream flavors more, with the exception of spearmint because it's the only one that's really different. I almost always got nectar cream, chocolate, ice cream. See all these fancy flavors—cause I'm old—like Tiger's Blood and Batman? I don't even know what that is. I like the basics.
>
> I like how they do it at Pandora's where they put the ice cream up to halfway, then they put more ice on it, put more flavor on it, and then do the top. So you get a little bit of ice cream on the top and as you eat through, there's ice cream in the middle. Stuffed is my favorite.
>
> —Victor Pizarro

**MY THOUGHTS:** This snowball stand is still pretty new, and I found the syrup to be more sweet than flavorful. I'm looking forward to visiting again, maybe before taking my son to the playground just down the block or after taking him to watch kids play ball at Milne Park.

# Van's
## Snoballs

4811 General Meyer Ave.
& 3052 Mercedes Blvd., New Orleans
(504) 400-2625

**My Order:** Root beer with condensed milk

**Details About Stand:** This sunny but shaded stand gets a little busy and is a Westbank favorite, having been around since 1976. One flavor I don't think you see anywhere else is the Tulane Green Wave. There's covered seating, ice cream snacks, and the expected snowball stand cuisine.

> Today I'm getting nachos and a wedding cake with strawberry cheesecake and condensed milk. I get the same thing every time, since I was a kid. And I grew up here, so I've been coming to Van's since I was about eight. During the hot days in the summer, I remember riding my bike from way down the street just to come get a snowball from over here. That used to be a long ride. Twenty minutes just to come here and get a snowball. Now it's me and my little brother, so whenever he wants nachos, I just get a snowball. Or when I work at the pool, I come get a snowball every day for work.

—THADDEUS MITCHELL

**MY THOUGHTS:** I love that Van's is across the street from Chubbie's Fried Chicken, and I think the flavors are all really good. My favorite part is that flavor combination suggestions are written on the menu for inspiration. And, speaking of inspiration, the "Have You Had a Snowball Today?" sign on General Meyer always makes me want to pull over.

# Who Want Some

7300 Read Blvd., New Orleans
(504) 491-9962
www.facebook.com/WhoWantSome

**My Order:** Coconut coffee snowball and ranch crawfish fries

**Details About Stand:** The stand is just a little shed, basically, with the things you'd expect from most stands. What sets this stand apart from many others, though, is the selection of specialty french fries and nachos and the big variety of flavors.

> " I like piña colada with everything else. Today I got piña colada and passion fruit. I usually go right there by Brother Martin, on Elysian Fields. And this is my first snowball since the spring, since I took it out of my diet. By the Brother Martin stand, I usually get piña colada or piña colada and watermelon. My dad used to always take us, every time. Besides that, it was like an afterschool treat when I used to get good grades or whatever. When I was a kid, all I knew at the time was bubble gum. But I went to piña colada in my twenties so I just stuck with it.
>
> –Jonathan Bloom "

**MY THOUGHTS:** I really enjoyed my crawfish ranch fries but will try a different snowball next time, like maybe the pink champagne.

# My Records
## on
## NEW ORLEANS SNOWBALL STANDS

| STAND: | MY ORDER: | MY THOUGHTS: |
|---|---|---|
| ABear's Snoball Stand<br>121 Westbank Expy.,<br>Westwego | | |
| Abracadabra Snowballs<br>1309 Lapalco Blvd.,<br>Westwego | | |
| Belle Chasse Dairy Dip<br>9252 Highway 23,<br>Belle Chasse | | |

| STAND: | MY ORDER: | MY THOUGHTS: |
|---|---|---|
| **Big Chief Snowballs**<br>1739 N. Galvez St.,<br>New Orleans | | |
| **The Big Chill**<br>2413 David Dr.,<br>Metairie | | |
| **Brain Freeze**<br>10816 Hayne Blvd.,<br>New Orleans | | |
| **Broad Street**<br>1703 N. Broad St.,<br>New Orleans | | |
| **Bubbie's Sno-Balls**<br>391 West Esplanade Ave.,<br>Kenner | | |

| STAND: | MY ORDER: | MY THOUGHTS: |
|---|---|---|
| **Buck's Sno-Wiz**<br>133 Westbank Expy.,<br>Westwego | | |
| **Casey's Snoblls**<br>4608 W. Esplanade Ave.,<br>Metairie | | |
| **Chilly's Snoballs**<br>3940 Veterans Blvd.,<br>Metairie | | |
| **Cold Spot**<br>2837 Barataria Blvd.,<br>Marrero | | |
| **Dino's Snowballs<br>& Ice Cream**<br>4524 S. I-10 Service Road W,<br>Metairie | | |

| STAND: | MY ORDER: | MY THOUGHTS: |
|---|---|---|
| **Flavors Snoballs**<br>500 Vintage Dr.,<br>Kenner | | |
| **The Frigid Zone**<br>2201 Lapalco Blvd.,<br>Harvey | | |
| **Galvez Goodies**<br>2036 Caffin Ave.,<br>New Orleans | | |
| **Goody's Sno-Balls**<br>2229 Palmisano Blvd.,<br>Chalmette | | |
| **Hansen's Sno-Bliz**<br>4801 Tchoupitoulas St.,<br>New Orleans | | |

| STAND: | MY ORDER: | MY THOUGHTS: |
|---|---|---|
| **Ike's Snowballs**<br>520 City Park Ave.,<br>New Orleans | | |
| **Imperial Woodpecker**<br>1 Poydras St., Spanish Plaza<br>& 3511 Magazine St.,<br>New Orleans | | |
| **Lickety Split's**<br>1043 Poland Ave.,<br>New Orleans | | |
| **Lou-Lou's Snoballs**<br>734 Papworth Ave.,<br>Metairie | | |
| **Mom & Pop Snowballs**<br>7479 St. Claude Ave.,<br>Arabi | | |

| STAND: | MY ORDER: | MY THOUGHTS: |
|---|---|---|
| Mr. Frank's Snoballs<br>2215 Hickory Ave.,<br>Harahan | | |
| NOLA Snow Snoballs<br>908 Harrison Ave.<br>& 7040 Vicksburg St.,<br>New Orleans | | |
| The Original New Orle-<br>ans Snoball & Smoothie<br>4339 Elysian Fields Ave.,<br>New Orleans | | |
| Pandora's Snowballs<br>901 N. Carrollton Ave.<br>New Orleans | | |
| Plum Street Snoballs<br>1300 Burdette St.,<br>New Orleans | | |

| STAND: | MY ORDER: | MY THOUGHTS: |
|---|---|---|
| **Pontilly Sno**<br>3968 Old Gentilly Rd.,<br>New Orleans | | |
| **Red Rooster Snowballs**<br>2801 Washington Ave.,<br>New Orleans | | |
| **River Breez Sno Balls**<br>4800 E. Saint Bernard Hwy.,<br>Violet | | |
| **Ro-Bear's**<br>6969 Jefferson Hwy.,<br>Harahan | | |
| **Rodney's**<br>9231 Lake Forest Blvd.,<br>New Orleans | | |

| STAND: | MY ORDER: | MY THOUGHTS: |
|---|---|---|
| Sal's Sno-Balls<br>1823 Metairie Road,<br>Metairie | | |
| Scuba Steve's<br>2400 Barataria Blvd.,<br>Marrero | | |
| Shivering Sam's<br>30 Westbank Expy.,<br>Gretna | | |
| Sno Shak<br>4001 Jefferson Hwy.,<br>Jefferson | | |
| Sno-La Snoball Lounge<br>2311 N. Causeway Blvd.,<br>Metairie & 8108 Hampson St.,<br>New Orleans | | |

| STAND: | MY ORDER: | MY THOUGHTS: |
|---|---|---|
| Snow World Snoballs<br>629 Berhman Hwy.,<br>Terrytown | | |
| SnoWizard<br>4001 Magazine St.,<br>New Orleans | | |
| Stop Jockin<br>3600 St. Bernard Ave.,<br>New Orleans | | |
| Sunny's<br>3437 Florida Ave.,<br>Kenner | | |
| Sweet Shack Snowballs<br>1716 Stumpf Blvd.,<br>Gretna | | |

| STAND: | MY ORDER: | MY THOUGHTS: |
|---|---|---|
| **Taft Park Snoballs**<br>3310 Taft Park,<br>Metairie | | |
| **Taste This! Snowballs**<br>5335 Venus St.,<br>New Orleans | | |
| **Van's**<br>4811 General Meyer Ave.<br>& 3052 Mercedes Blvd.,<br>Algiers | | |
| **Who Want Some**<br>7300 Read Blvd.,<br>New Orleans | | |

# ADDITIONAL NOTES & NEW STANDS:

**Crescent City Snow** is part guidebook, part diary, and part biography of fifty snowball stands and their customers in the greater New Orleans area. Keep a copy of *Crescent City Snow* in the car for when you want to try a new place, and use the table in the back to record your own observations. Make sure to visit CrescentCitySnow.com and follow @CrescentCitySnow on Facebook and Instagram.

**Megan Braden-Perry** is a native New Orleanian, Dillard University alum, and mother of a three-year-old boy named Franklin. She's highly motivated by food and drink and, according to her friend Jenny Martin, "will talk to the devil for a sandwich." Aside from eating and drinking, she enjoys attending cultural and political events, often with her son, as to "train up a child" in hopes he'll do the right thing and attend an HBCU. She's been published in *Essence*, *NY Daily News*, *Jezebel*, NOLA.com | *The Times-Picayune*, *Gambit*, and *Where Magazine*. She is also the author of the children's book, *Allen the Alligator Counts Through New Orleans*.